Piano Solos

Book 2

Authors
**Barbara Kreader,
Fred Kern, Phillip Keveren**

Consultants
Mona Rejino, Tony Caramia,
Bruce Berr, Richard Rejino

*Director,
Educational Keyboard Publications*
Margaret Otwell

Editor
Anne Wester

Illustrator
Fred Bell

FOREWORD

Piano Solos presents challenging original music that coordinates page-by-page with the **Piano Lessons** and **Piano Practice Games** books in the **Hal Leonard Student Piano Library**. The outstanding variety of composers and musical styles makes every solo an important piece in its own right – exciting to both performer and listener. In addition, each piece is designed to encourage and ensure further mastery of the concepts and skills in the **Piano Lessons** books.

May these **Piano Solos** become favorite pieces that delight all who hear and play them.

Best wishes,

Book: ISBN 978-0-7935-6267-1
Book/CD: ISBN 978-0-634-08981-7

HAL•LEONARD®
CORPORATION

7777 W. BLUEMOUND RD. P.O. BOX 13819 MILWAUKEE, WI 53213

Visit Hal Leonard Online at
www.halleonard.com

Piano Solos Book 2

CONTENTS

*✔

* Students can check pieces as they play them.

Magnet March

Stepping steady

Phillip Keveren

Accompaniment (Student plays one octave higher than written.)

Stepping steady (♩ = 120)

mf detached

Use with Lesson Book 2, pg. 7

Song Of The Orca

Singing, with mystery

Phillip Keveren

Come and play with me, Jes - sie, Jes - sie.

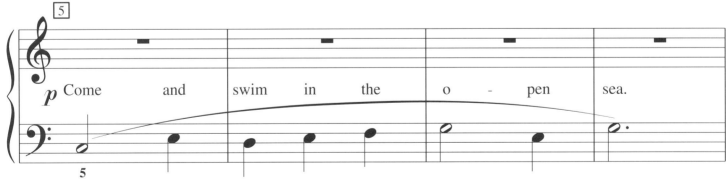

Come and swim in the o - pen sea.

Accompaniment (Student plays two octaves higher than written.)

Singing, with mystery (♩=125)

9 *mf* Ride with me to our se - cret is - land.

13 *p* Jes - sie, Jes - sie, *mf* come and play in the sea.

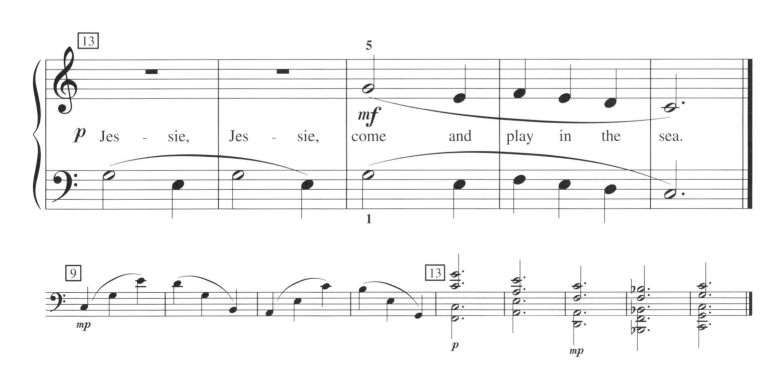

The Macaroni Cha-Cha

Phillip Keveren

With gusto

We love chees-y mac-a - ro - ni, We real - ly

LOVE that chees-y mac-a - ro - ni. (Cha-cha - cha.) Well,

Accompaniment (Student plays one octave higher than written.)

With gusto (♩ = 190)

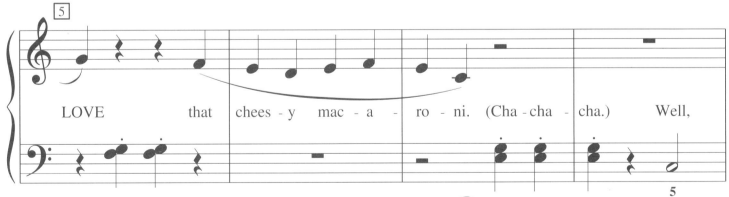

The Stream

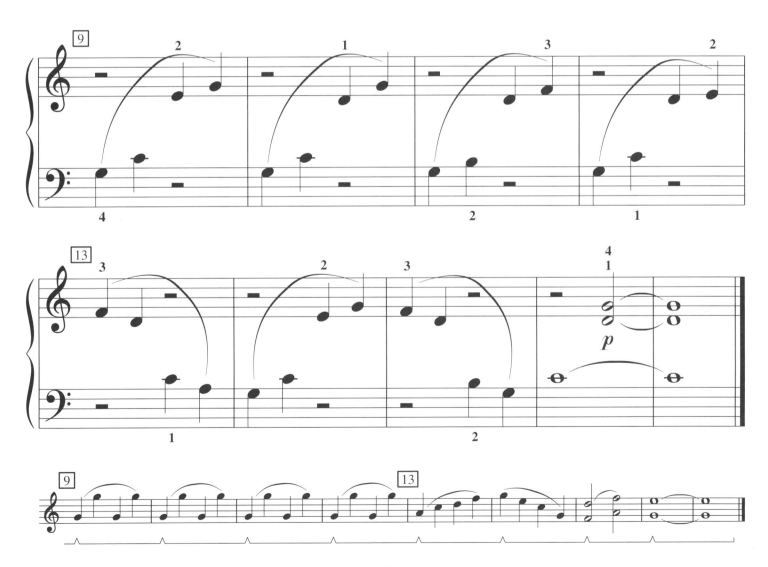

Leaps And Bounds

Moderato (♩ = 155) **9/10** **5**

Italo Taranta

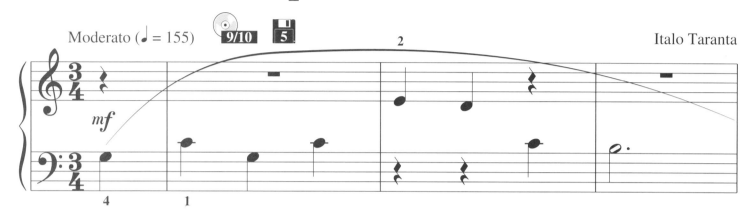

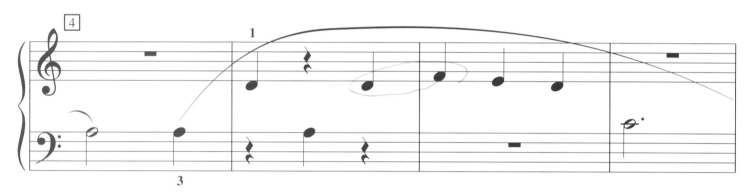

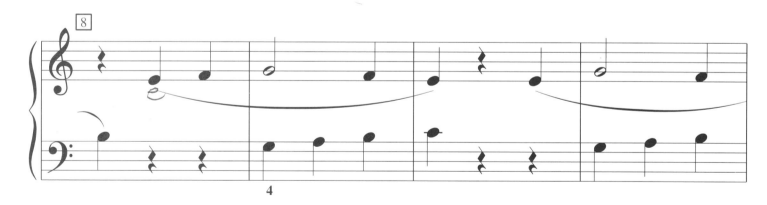

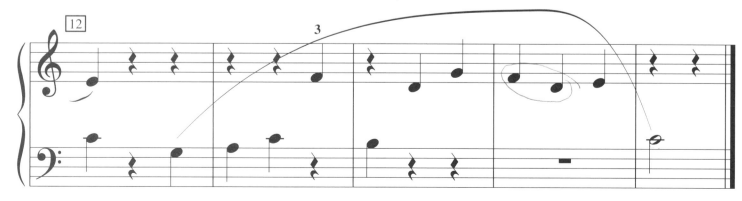

Use with Lesson Book 2, pg. 15

Tender Dialogue

Italo Taranta

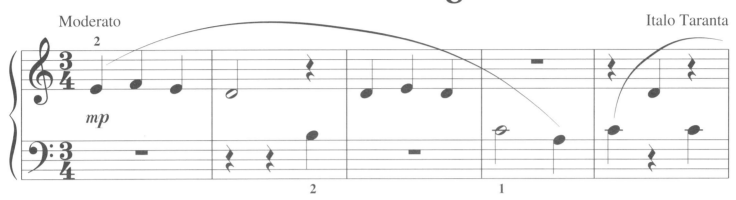

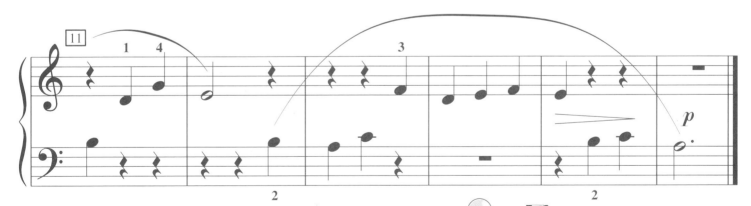

Accompaniment (Student plays one octave higher than written.)

Use with Lesson Book 2, pg. 16

Dance Of The Court Jester

With humor

Bill Boyd

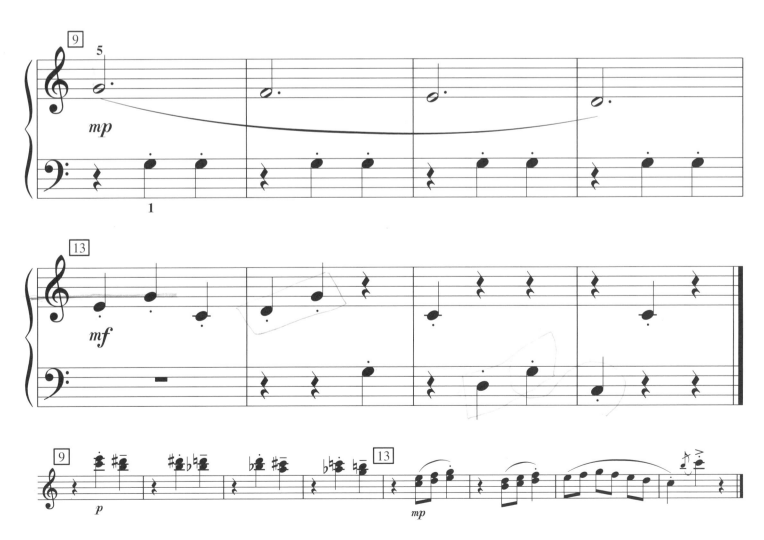

Tribal Celebration

blackkeys

Medium fast

Christos Tsitsaros

Accompaniment (Student plays one octave higher than written.) **15/16** **8**

Medium fast (♩ = 200)

mp drum-like

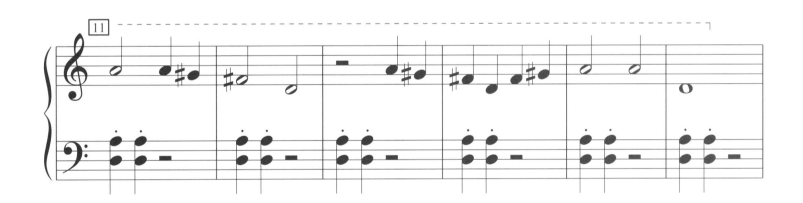

* When the sign *loco* appears, play the notes where written.

The Accompaniment

Student Accompaniment
With energy

Bill Boyd

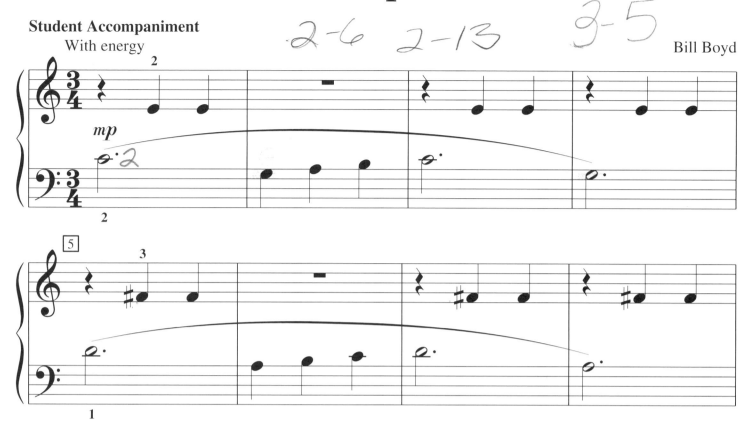

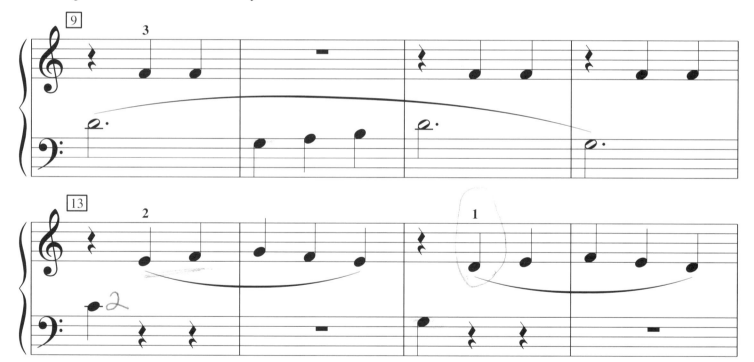

A sharp before a note lasts for only one measure.

Teacher Solo (Student plays one octave lower than written. Teacher may play one octave higher than written.)

With energy (♩ = 175)

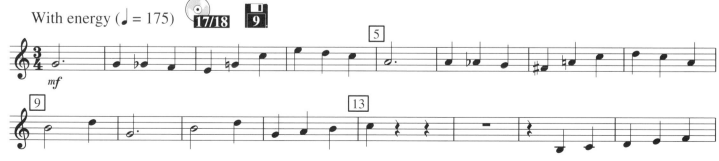

move hand ①

Take It Slow

3/19 3/26

Slowly (♩ = 85)

Bill Boyd

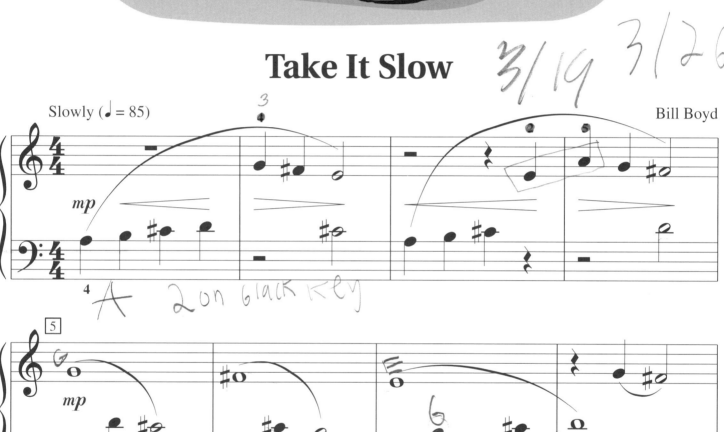

A 2 on black key

Accompaniment (Student plays one octave higher than written.) 🔘**19/20** 💾**10**

Slowly (♩ = 85)

simile

With pedal

Viva La Rhumba!

Allegro

Carol Klose

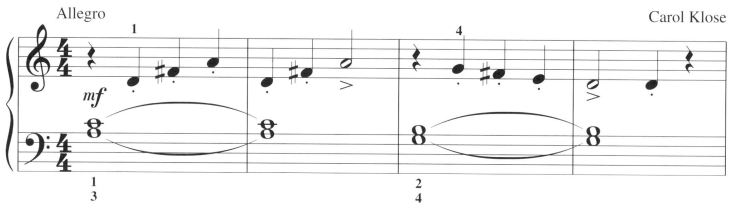

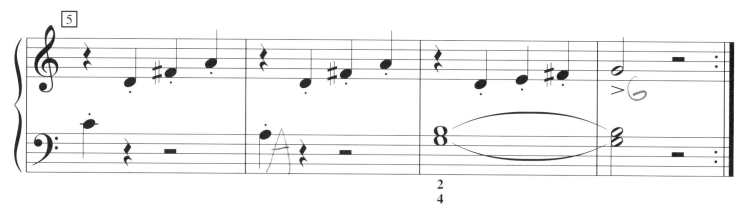

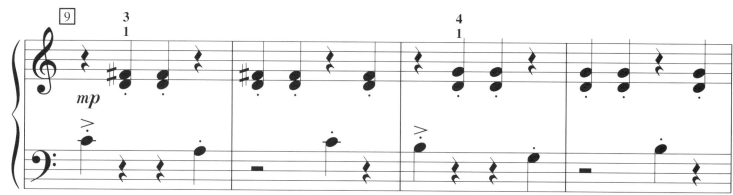

Accompaniment (Student plays one octave higher than written.)

Allegro (♩ = 120)

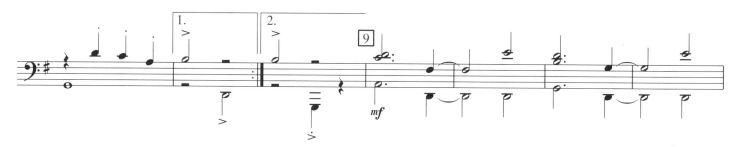

Grandmother's Lace

Flowing Waltz tempo

Carol Klose

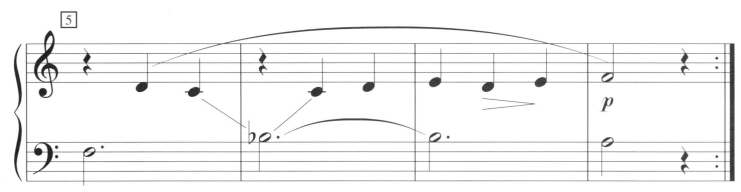

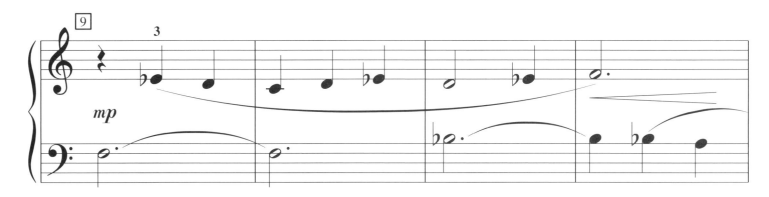

Accompaniment (Student plays one octave higher than written.) **23/24** **12**

Flowing Waltz tempo (♩ = 140)

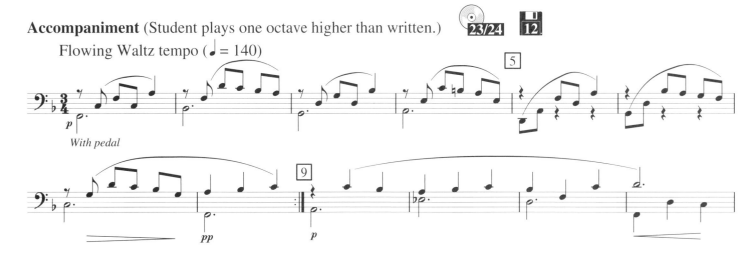

With pedal

Those Creepy Crawly Things
On The Cellar Floor

Stepping very carefully (♩ = 140) **25/26** **13**

Carol Klose

L.H. 8va lower throughout

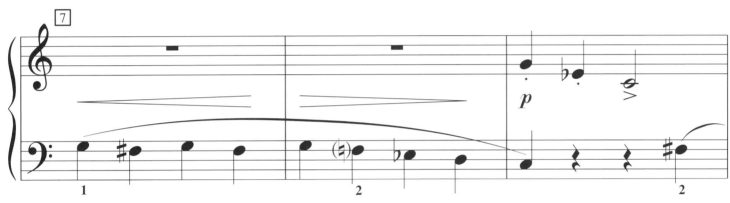

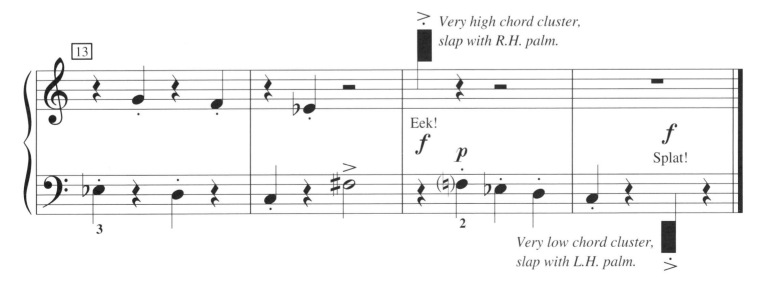

Very high chord cluster, slap with R.H. palm.

Eek!

Splat!

Very low chord cluster, slap with L.H. palm.

On Fourth Avenue

Leisurely, not fast (♩ = 120)

Fred Kern

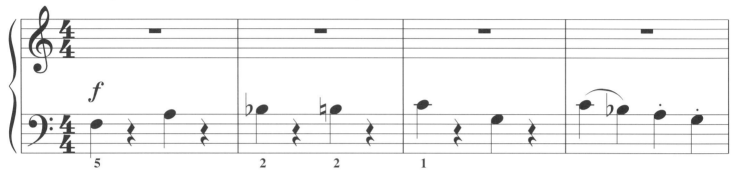

L.H. 8va lower throughout

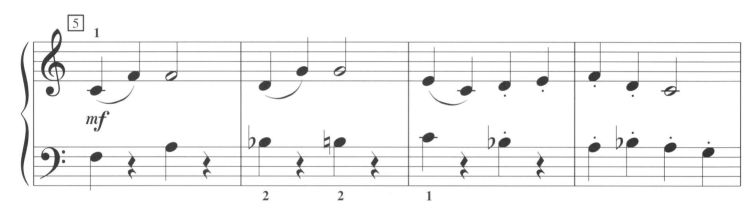

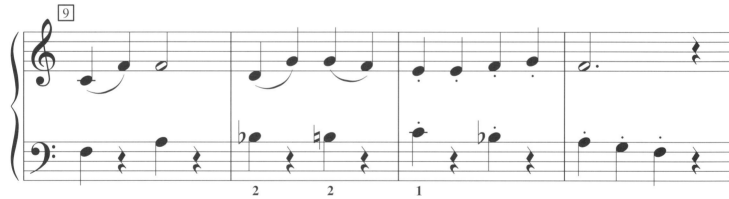

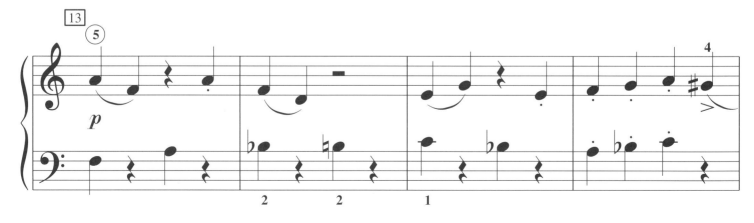

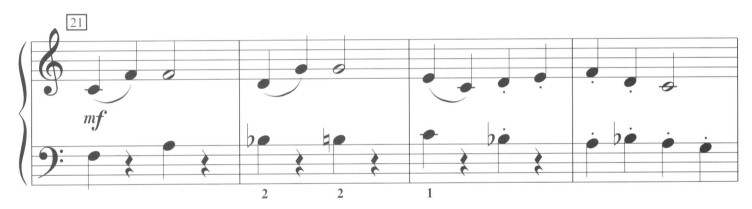

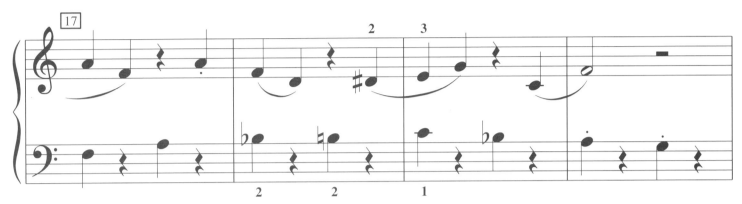

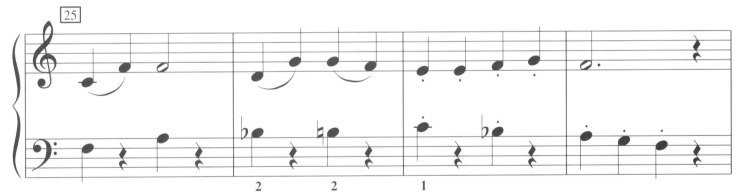

two octaves lower -

Goofy Gadget

Sputtering along steadily (♩ = 200)
Both hands 8va lower throughout

Phillip Keveren

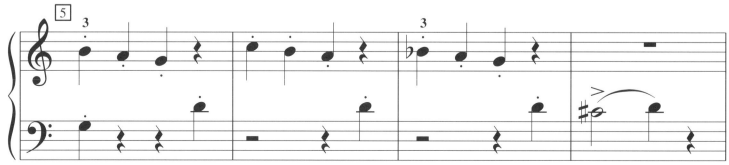

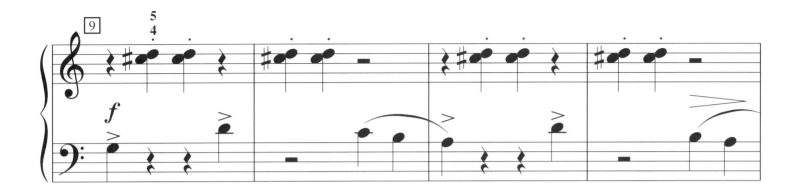

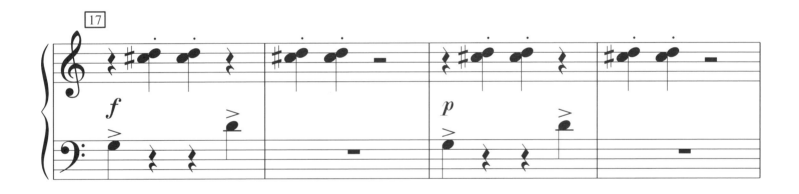

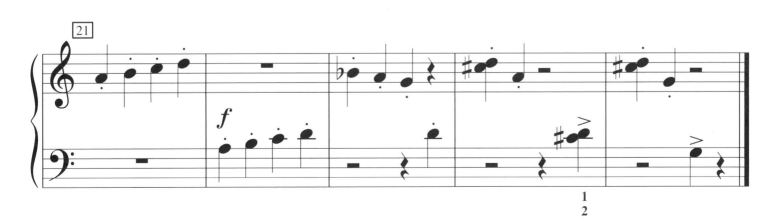

School Is Out!

Fast Pop/Rock beat (♩ = 200) **31/32** **16**

Barbara Gallagher

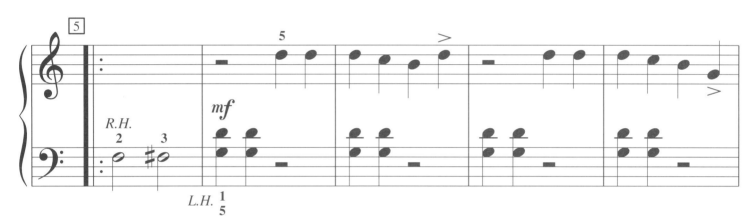

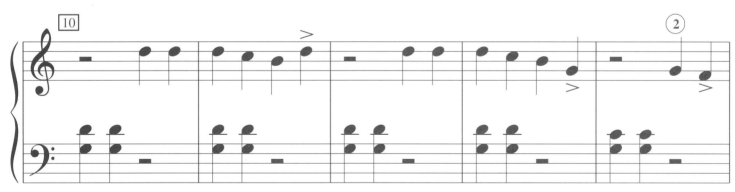

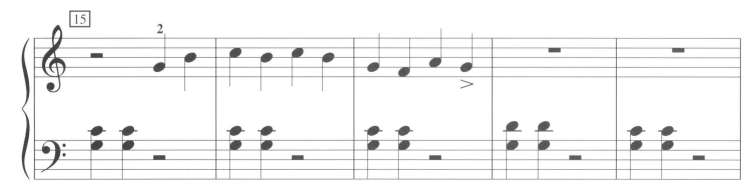

Use with Lesson Book 2, pg. 45

COMPOSER SHOWCASE
HAL LEONARD STUDENT PIANO LIBRARY

This series showcases great original piano music from our **Hal Leonard Student Piano Library** family of composers, including Bill Boyd, Phillip Keveren, Carol Klose, Jennifer Linn, Mona Rejino, Eugénie Rocherolle and more. Carefully graded for easy selection, each book contains gems that are certain to become tomorrow's classics!

BILL BOYD

JAZZ BITS (AND PIECES)
Early Intermediate Level
00290312 11 Solos.............................$6.99

JAZZ DELIGHTS
Intermediate Level
00240435 11 Solos.............................$7.99

JAZZ FEST
Intermediate Level
00240436 10 Solos.............................$7.99

JAZZ PRELIMS
Early Elementary Level
00290032 12 Solos.............................$6.99

JAZZ SKETCHES
Intermediate Level
00220001 8 Solos.............................$6.99

JAZZ STARTERS
Elementary Level
00290425 10 Solos.............................$6.99

JAZZ STARTERS II
Late Elementary Level
00290434 11 Solos.............................$7.99

JAZZ STARTERS III
Late Elementary Level
00290465 12 Solos.............................$7.99

THINK JAZZ!
Early Intermediate Level
00290417 Method Book.............$10.99

TONY CARAMIA

JAZZ MOODS
Intermediate Level
00296728 8 Solos.............................$6.95

SUITE DREAMS
Intermediate Level
00296775 4 Solos.............................$6.99

SONDRA CLARK

DAKOTA DAYS
Intermediate Level
00296521 5 Solos.............................$6.95

FAVORITE CAROLS FOR TWO
Intermediate Level
00296530 5 Duets.............................$7.99

FLORIDA FANTASY SUITE
Intermediate Level
00296766 3 Duets.............................$7.95

ISLAND DELIGHTS
Intermediate Level
00296666 4 Solos.............................$6.95

THREE ODD METERS
Intermediate Level
00296472 3 Duets.............................$6.95

MATTHEW EDWARDS

CONCERTO FOR YOUNG PIANISTS
FOR 2 PIANOS, FOUR HANDS
Intermediate Level Book/CD
00296356 3 Movements $16.95

CONCERTO NO. 2 IN G MAJOR
FOR 2 PIANOS, 4 HANDS
Intermediate Level Book/CD
00296670 3 Movements.............$16.95

PHILLIP KEVEREN

MOUSE ON A MIRROR
Late Elementary Level
00296361 5 Solos.............................$6.95

MUSICAL MOODS
Elementary/Late Elementary Level
00296714 7 Solos.............................$5.95

ROMP! – BOOK/CD PACK
A DIGITAL KEYBOARD ENSEMBLE FOR SIX PLAYERS
Intermediate Level
00296549 Book/CD.............................$9.95
00296548 Book/GM Disk $9.95

SHIFTY-EYED BLUES
Late Elementary Level
00296374 5 Solos.............................$6.99

TEX-MEX REX
Late Elementary Level
00296353 6 Solos.............................$5.95

CAROL KLOSE

CORAL REEF SUITE
Late Elementary Level
00296354 7 Solos.............................$6.99

DESERT SUITE
Intermediate Level
00296667 6 Solos.............................$7.99

FANCIFUL WALTZES
Early Intermediate Level
00296473 5 Solos.............................$7.95

GARDEN TREASURES
Late Intermediate Level
00296787 5 Solos.............................$7.99

TRADITIONAL CAROLS FOR TWO
Late Elementary Level
00296557 5 Duets.............................$7.99

WATERCOLOR MINIATURES
Early Intermediate Level
00296848 7 Solos.............................$7.99

JENNIFER LINN

AMERICAN IMPRESSIONS
Intermediate Level
00296471 6 Solos.............................$7.99

CHRISTMAS IMPRESSIONS
Intermediate Level
00296706 8 Solos.............................$6.99

JUST PINK
Elementary Level
00296722 9 Solos.............................$6.99

LES PETITES IMAGES
Late Elementary Level
00296664 7 Solos.............................$7.99

LES PETITES IMPRESSIONS
Intermediate Level
00296355 6 Solos.............................$7.99

REFLECTIONS
Late Intermediate Level
00296843 5 Solos.............................$7.99

FOR MORE INFORMATION, SEE YOUR LOCAL MUSIC DEALER,
OR WRITE TO:

HAL•LEONARD®
CORPORATION

7777 W. BLUEMOUND RD. P.O. BOX 13819 MILWAUKEE, WI 53213

For full descriptions and song lists for the books listed here, and to view a complete list of titles in this series, please visit our website at www.halleonard.com

TALES OF MYSTERY
Intermediate Level
00296769 6 Solos.............................$7.99

MONA REJINO

CIRCUS SUITE
Late Elementary Level
00296665 5 Solos.............................$5.95

JUST FOR KIDS
Elementary Level
00296840 8 Solos.............................$7.99

MERRY CHRISTMAS MEDLEYS
Intermediate Level
00296799 5 Solos.............................$7.99

PORTRAITS IN STYLE
Early Intermediate Level
00296507 6 Solos.............................$7.99

EUGÉNIE ROCHEROLLE

JAMBALAYA
FOR 2 PIANOS, 8 HANDS
Intermediate Level
00296654 Piano Ensemble.............$9.99

JAMBALAYA
FOR 2 PIANOS, 4 HANDS
Intermediate Level
00296725 Piano Duo (2 Pianos) $7.95

TOUR FOR TWO
Late Elementary Level
00296832 6 Duets.............................$7.99

CHRISTOS TSITSAROS

DANCES FROM AROUND THE WORLD
Early Intermediate Level
00296688 7 Solos.............................$6.95

POETIC MOMENTS
Intermediate Level
00296403 8 Solos.............................$7.95

SONATINA HUMORESQUE
Late Intermediate Level
00296772 3 Movements $6.99

SONGS WITHOUT WORDS
Intermediate Level
00296506 9 Solos.............................$7.95

THROUGHOUT THE YEAR
Late Elementary Level
00296723 12 Duets.............................$6.95

ADDITIONAL COLLECTIONS

AMERICAN PORTRAITS
by Wendy Stevens
Intermediate Level
00296817 6 Solos.............................$7.99

**MONDAY'S CHILD
(A CHILD'S BLESSINGS)**
by Deborah Brady
Intermediate Level
00296373 7 Solos.............................$6.95

PLAY THE BLUES!
by Luann Carman (Method Book)
Early Intermediate Level
00296357 10 Solos.............................$8.99

PUPPY DOG TALES
by Deborah Brady
Elementary Level
00296718 5 Solos.............................$6.95

WORLD GEMS
FOR 2 PIANOS, 8 HANDS
arr. by Amy O'Grady
Early Intermediate Level
00296505 6 Folk Songs $6.95